The
Everlastings

BOOKS BY NORMAN DUBIE

The Everlastings

NORMAN DUBIE

DOUBLEDAY & COMPANY, INC.
Garden City, New York

1980

Grateful acknowledgment is made to the following publications in which these poems first appeared:

The Agni Review: *The Sketchbook Ashes of Jehoshaphat.*

The American Poetry Review: *Double Sphere, Cloven Sphere; The Night Before Thanksgiving; Ode to the Spectral Thief, Alpha; The Parallax Monograph for Rodin;* and *The Everlastings.*

Antaeus: *Grand Illusion.*

Crazyhorse: *Lord Myth; Not the Cuckold's Dream.*

The Gramercy Review: *Against the Wishbone; Empiricists of Crimson; Telemachos Who Believes Ulysses Is the Night* and *The Circus Ringmaster's Apology to God.*

Field: *The Composer's Winter Dream; Coleridge Crossing the Plain of Jars.*

The New Yorker: *The Fox Who Watched for the Midnight Sun* (p. 11) and *The Land of Cockaigne: 1568* (p. 31) copyright © 1978 by The New Yorker Magazine, Inc., and *Principia Mathematica: Einstein's Exile in an Old Dutch Winter* (p. 67), copyright © 1979 by The New Yorker Magazine, Inc., were reprinted by permission.

Poetry (Chicago): *The World Isn't a Wedding of the Artists of Yesterday* and *The Scrivener's Roses.*

Porch: *There Is a Dream Dreaming Us* and *After Spring Snow, What They Saw.*

The Seneca Review: *Comes Winter, The Sea Hunting.*

Excerpt from *Renoir, My Father* by Jean Renoir. Copyright © 1958, 1962 by Jean Renoir. Reprinted by permission of Little, Brown and Company and the William Morris Agency. Excerpt from "The First Morning of the Second World" in *Summer Knowledge* by Delmore Schwartz. Copyright © 1955 by Delmore Schwartz. Reprinted by permission of Doubleday & Company, Inc.

Library of Congress Cataloging in Publication Data

Dubie, Norman, 1945–
The everlastings.

I. Title.
PS3554.U255E9   811'.5'4
This edition appears in hardcover and softcover
ISBN: 0-385-15329-5 Trade
0-385-15330-9 Paperbound
Library of Congress Catalog Card Number 79–7624

For Michael Burkard

Notes:

Grand Illusion was written in memory of Earl Morrill, Jr., *Principia Mathematica: Einstein's Exile in an Old Dutch Winter* is for the Goldensohns, and *The Everlastings* is in memory of Merle Brown. The entoiled ringmaster in *The Circus Ringmaster's Apology to God* has his origin in Bergman's *The Naked Night*.

This book was written while I enjoyed a grant from the John Simon Guggenheim Memorial Foundation to whom a grateful acknowledgment is made.

Contents

ONE

TWO

The
Everlastings

ONE

Grand Illusion

My father had several times expressed a fear of being
buried alive. I insisted that the doctor should do
whatever was necessary. The doctor asked me to leave
the room. When I came back, he was able to assure
me that Renoir was dead!

                                    —JEAN RENOIR

It is not 1937 for long. A clump of ash trees and a walk
Down to the boathouse: inside linen is tacked up
In a long blank mural; the children sit on the wings
Of the dry-dock, and then, over the water in a circle
Of rowboats, the aunts and uncles wait while
At their center the projectionist, Jean Renoir,
On a cedar raft, casts silhouettes of rabbits, birds
And turtles for the sleepy children. Corks
Come out of old bottles, it is a few minutes past sunset
And, now, a swimmer beside the raft looks

Into the boathouse to the linens: *at last, it is 1915!*
A bird screams over the lake, two bats
Flitter back and forth through the beam of the lamp,
Interrupting the images, the grand illusion, cast over
Water to the acceptance of white tablecloths
On the darkening shore of the lake. A torch is lit
For its kerosene smoke is repugnant to the swarming insects.
This film and its prisoners exist between extreme borders,
Not music and algebra, but
A war, and then, yet another war . . .

But we begin with the captured officers digging
A tunnel that will soon be outside the garden wall.
The Boches observe the Frenchmen working
With their hoes as from the trousers of a boy
Dirt from the tunnel secretly spills onto horse manure!
The prisoners dream of crossing a meadow filled
With snow, in the moonlight it is jade-green snow
While Germans with rifles on a hill
Are unable to kill them, for they have escaped
Into Switzerland with its feather-brushed trees

And patina of copper roof-tops along a hillside village.
Isn't this the ending of the film?
No! I'm sorry but
There is a single blossom
On the geranium, and when it falls, Captain de Boeldieu
Dies, discovering his afterlife along a November road—
He does not know that two men are hiding in the marsh
Beside him; nevertheless, it is at this moment that the film
Suffers its true conclusion. The two men hiding
In the marsh will escape across the border, only
To be returned to the continuing war. This is why there
Is no importance to your version of the story. And there
Will be another war. And more horror for the geranium!
So, to pass the time, the imprisoned soldiers receive
A steamer trunk filled with women's clothing.
They will all perform in a revue: a chorus
Of boys and men, rouge and talcum, black stockings,
Garters, the *tonneau* dresses, false breasts and
Large paper carnations riding up like epaulets

On their broad shoulders. These poignant inversions
Are not ridiculous, the third boy from the right
Has delicate milky thighs, these women are not ridiculous
Until they begin to stiffen into men as they sing,
In this comedy, their national anthem! The Russian

Prisoners have been given a trunk, also, from their
Mysterious Tsarina; the men open it expecting vodka
And sausages. The box is filled with straw
And books on cooking, painting and algebra. In disgust
They burn these books— kiss good-bye the frontier

Of algebra and the desire for wedding tripe!
Now, these officers who are escape-artists are moved
As an elite corps and north to Wintersborn. Later,
They are taken to a damp limestone castle
From which no one will escape. The Commandant
Is the stoic aristocrat, Rauffenstein, his head is in
A brace like a white egg in a silver teaspoon.
I mean no disrespect, but the balding Rauffenstein is
An abject picture of suffering. His villa has but one
Flower, a tall laden geranium.

Rauffenstein and the other aristocrat, Boeldieu,
Are friends. Both would know that to clear a monocle
One uses spirits of vinegar. They stand confirmed
In manner beside a squirrel cage. Rauffenstein feels
Superior to the other two principals, the rich
Jew, Rosenthal, and the charming emotional Marechal.
These two hide in the marsh while Boeldieu dies
Of a bullet wound. Only a king may kill a king!
And Rauffenstein did it with his pistol; taking aim
But missing the leg; he severed in three places,
                              Boeldieu's intestine!

The Captain is given a room in the turret that holds
The flowering geranium. Now comes the *oratio obliqua*
Of the marksman, Rauffenstein; the disfigured Commandant
Is sincerely saddened
At having killed the noble Captain. But before
The shooting and escape we sensed the Captain's
Sacrifice was not sacrifice, or suicide, but

The grand escape— a country road into another landscape . . .
There are bells tolling down in the village.
Rosenthal and Marechal with ropes have dropped

Past the castle's battlements to the ground.
They run away across snowy farmland. Marechal's teeth
Are stained from chewing licorice flavored tobacco.
Rosenthal and Marechal are extremes who have
Strong feelings for each other. They are befriended
By a German widow, Ulsa, and her daughter, Lotte;
Ulsa sleeps with the tall handsome Jew. He promises
To return for her when the war is over. He
Will lose both his legs at Mégéglise.
This is not known within the story, but he'll bleed

To death beside a little bridge. He lived his illusion
In the orient of Delacroix, his servants were Syrians
And Negroes. He loved the little ivory spoons that
Chinese women in the open markets use to bathe
And freshen the exotic tiny fish they sell out
Of huge clay bowls . . .
In the boathouse the children sleep, while Jean's
Oldest cousin, drunken, falls out of a rowboat.
The lone swimmer has joined Renoir on the raft.
The film now reveals the *first diversion*
As all of the prisoners of the fortress begin playing
Several hundred wooden flutes, the noise is like women
Crying over the fresh mounds at Verdun. This diversion
Is not illusion
And as the Boches collect the flutes, the drunken cousin
Tries to join Renoir on the raft. Boeldieu flees
To the heights of the castle, the second diversion!
We hear: *Halt! Halt! Halt!*
A gunshot, and chowder with blood falls from Boeldieu's
Opened stomach all the way down to the courtyard.

There are small fish bones in the viscera on the cobbled
Courtyard floor. Scissors cut the blue blossom
From the geranium. Boeldieu will die . . .   dead,
He awakens on a country road where, now a peasant,
He walks a white horse under the looming, bare trees.
Rosenthal and Marechal are watching
As they hide in the dead marsh flowers of
An early November. They are alive. They do not
Recognize their friend. Renoir's cousin, asking for
More wine, climbing onto the raft, spills

Everything, and the projector with its crude lamp
Sinks slowly to the bottom of the lake—
Its dusky lighted windows like a bathysphere
Lost off a cable that frayed, whoever is alive
Inside the iron bell is experiencing
An eternal falling through water without the promise
Of a bottom . . .   it's 1937, the children
Asleep in the boathouse are being aroused, they wake
To a bat caught in the wall of linen, they think it's
Their uncle still casting images of animals for them . . .

Double Sphere, Cloven Sphere

The black clouds swell up around the setting sun
Making a distant elm conspicuous,
Its rosy domination like the claw

On a garden rake held up
Before the face and through which
The blinking leaf-fires of late autumn play.

The blue sheafs
Of tree shadows fall across the doorway where
A man and a woman are speaking, looking at their feet,
In the yard full of leaves.

He repeats a simple sentence. The long sleeves
Of her gray sweater will swallow her hands
As she dances a little in place, cold and impatient!

But they are both in pain.

A wet December day has made their naked bodies linger
Like red berries in the memory.

It ends over white papers with a stranger
Who awards the man two chairs, who awards the woman
A sofa and mirror.

They begin to walk away, in opposite directions,
Kicking up leaves—tears down their faces . . .

This farewell was both simple and difficult.
The incalculable
Ditches in the field below their cold house
Are touched with mist; ice

Forms in the stubble. *These were our times.*

And the slumbering ruse of early winter
Points a long finger in the direction
Of our exile:
                     a passage that's all so clear
Taking us over the horizon into atmosphere . . .

The Fox Who Watched
for the Midnight Sun

Across the snowy pastures of the estate
Open snares drift like pawprints under rain, everywhere
There is the conjured rabbit being dragged
Up into blowing snow: it struggles
Upside down by a leg, its belly
Is the slaked white of cottages along the North Sea.

Inside the parlor Ibsen writes of a summer garden, of a
Butterfly sunken inside the blossoming tulip.
He describes the snapdragon with its little sconce of dew.
He moves from the desk to a window. Remembers his studies
In medicine, picturing the sticky
Overlapping eyelids of drowned children. On the corner
Of the sofa wrapped in Empress-silks there's a box
Of fresh chocolates. He mimics the deceptively distant,
Chittering birdsong within the cat's throat.
How it attracts finches to her open window.
He turns toward the fire, now thinking of late sessions in Storting.
Ibsen had written earlier of an emotional girl
With sunburnt shoulders,

Her surprise when the heavy dipper came up
From the well with frogs' eggs bobbing in her water.
He smiles.

Crosses the room like the fox walking away
From the woodpile.
He picks up his lamp and takes it
To the soft chair beneath the window. Brandy is poured.
Weary, he closes his eyes and dreams
Of his mother at a loom, how she would dip, dressing
The warp with a handful of coarse wool.

Henrik reaches for tobacco—   tomorrow, he'll write
Of summer some more, he'll begin with a fragrance . . .
Now, though, he wonders about the long
Devotion of his muscles to his bones. He's worried by
The wind which hurries the pages in this drafty room.
He looks out
Into the March storm for an illustration: under a tree
A large frozen hare swings at the end of a snare-string.
The fox sits beneath it, his upturned head swinging with it,
The jaws are locked in concentration,

As if the dead hare were soon to awaken!

The Composer's Winter Dream

Vivid and heavy, he strolls through dark brick kitchens
Within the great house of Esterhazy:
A deaf servant's candle
Is tipped toward bakers who are quarreling about
The green kindling! The wassail is
Being made by pouring beer and sherry from dusty bottles

Over thirty baked apples in a large bowl: into
The wassail, young girls empty their aprons of
Cinnamon, ground mace and allspice berries. A cook adds
Egg whites and brandy. The giant, glass snifters
On a silver tray are taken from the kitchens by two maids.
The anxious pianist eats just the edges of a fig

Stuffed with Devonshire cream. In the sinks the gall bladders
Of geese are soaking in cold salted water.
Walking in the storm, this evening, he passed
Children in rags, singing carols; they were roped together
In the drifting snow outside the palace gate.
He knew he would remember those boys' faces . . .

There's a procession into the kitchens: larger boys, each
With a heavy shoe of coal. The pianist sits and looks
Hard at a long black sausage. He will not eat

Before playing the new sonata. Beside him
The table sags with hams, kidney pies and two shoulders
Of lamb. *A hand rings a bell in the parlour!*

No longer able to hide, he walks
Straight into the large room that blinds him with light.
He sits before the piano still thinking of hulled berries . . .
The simple sonata which

He is playing has little
To do with what he's feeling: something larger
Where a viola builds, in air, an infinite staircase.
An oboe joins the viola, they struggle
For a more florid harmony.
But the silent violins now emerge,

And like the big wing of a bird, smother everything
In a darkness from which only a single horn escapes—
Successively but in strict imitation of the viola
That feels effaced by the composer's dream . . .
But he is not dreaming,
The composer is finishing two performances simultaneously!

He is back in the dark kitchens, sulking and counting
His few florins—   they have paid him
With a snuff-box that was pressed
With two diamonds, in Holland!
This century discovers quinine.
And the sketchbooks of a mad, sad musician

Who threw a lantern at his landlord who was standing beside
A critic. He screamed: *here, take a snuff-box, I've filled
It with the dander of dragons!* He apologizes
The next morning, instructing the landlord to take
This *stuff* (Da Ist Der Wisch) to a publisher,
And sell it! *You'll have your velvet garters, Pig!*

The composer is deaf, loud and feverish . . . he went
To the countryside in a wet sedan-chair.
He said to himself: for the piper, seventy ducats! He'd curse
While running his fingers through his tousled hair, he made
The poor viola climb the stairs.
He desired loquats, loquats with small pears!

Ludwig, there are Spring-bears under the pepper trees!
The picnic by the stone house . . .   the minnows
Could have been sunlight striking fissures
In the stream; Ludwig, where your feet are
In the cold stream
Everything is horizontal like the land and living.

The stream sang, "In the beginning was the word
And without the word
Was not anything made that was made . . .
But let us believe in the word, Ludwig,
For it is like the sea grasses
Off which the giant snails eat, at twilight!" But then

The dream turns to autumn; the tinctures he
Swallows are doing nothing for him, and he shows
The physicians his spoon which has dissolved
In the mixtures the chemist has given him!
After the sonata was heard; the standing for applause
Over, he walked out where it was snowing.

It had been dark early that evening. It's here that the
Dream becomes shocking: he sees a doctor
In white sleeves
Who is sawing at the temporal bones of his ears. There is
A bag of dampened plaster for the death mask. And
Though he *is* dead, a pool of urine runs to the

Middle of the sickroom. A brass urinal is on the floor, it is
The shape of his ears rusting on gauze. The doctors

Drink stale wassail. They frown over the dead Beethoven. Outside,
The same March storm that swept through Vienna just an hour before
Has turned in its tracks like the black, caged panther
On exhibit in the Esterhazys' candlelit ballroom. The storm crosses
Over Vienna once more: lightning strikes the Opera House, its eaves
And awnings filled with hailstones,
Flames leaping to the adjacent stables! Someone had known,
As thunder dropped flower-boxes off window sills,
    Someone *must* have known
That, at this moment, the violins would emerge
    in a struggle with the loud, combatant horns . . .

The Night Before Thanksgiving

A grove of deep sycamores drifts into the Hudson,
The blue lights on a sledge
Go white as it drags its iron nets
Slowly up the trench of the river:
Inside an old Studebaker, my father sits beside a meadow.
Next to him there's a hot thermos, and a little box
Of codeine tablets for the pain in his knee. He reaches
Over into the backseat for a red, plaid blanket, it has
White hair on it from a long-dead cat. The blanket

Goes over his lap—   at that moment, a giant
Spectacle-moth settles like a falling hazel leaf on the blanket:
The moth, powdered in lime and chalk, has a lurid green
Eye on each forewing: it has come to my father after
A long season of feeding
From the night-flowering sweet tobacco!
The spectacle-moth has settled and died, and there is
The smell of burning gasoline.   On the river, a horn blows
Twice from a lamp-room that is followed by barges loaded
With coal; flames from a foundry climb over pine trees that
Are miles down the road . . .
Across the water there are lanterns
Over the lawns of a mansion where women

In long gowns are playing croquet without wickets. These women
Are drinking; they laugh and wave to
The lonely, bored man in the tug-boat who pulls on the horn, again.
My father waves to him; the moth closes
Its shattered ice-green eyes like a blackened coal miner
Stepping out of a mountain into the winter daylight . . .

Ode to the
Spectral Thief, Alpha

The stream silent as if empty. Dusk in the mirrors. Doors
                                    shutting.
Only one woman without a pitcher remains in the garden—
Made of water, transparent in moonlight, a flower in her hair!

—YANNIS RITSOS

The way grapes will cast a green rail,
With tendrils and flowers, out along
A broken fence, down the edge of a field;
Then, climbing over hawthorn and up
Into the low branches of an elm. The moon

Is also up in the branches of the elm along with
A raccoon who sits and fills himself
On the dark, dusty fruit—   under the branch,
On which the raccoon is situated,
His deep brown feces splatter over
Queen Anne's Lace and the waving sedge
Of the pond . . .

An owl lifts out of the tufted, solitary orchard
And there are hot-silver zig-zags, lightning
Up in the fat black clouds; this quiet
Before an August storm is nothing at all
Compared to the calm after a snowfall . . .
But the long boxes of hay in the field
Will stand, they are dense coffins
In which small living things

Are caught, broken: mouse, grasshopper,
And the lame sparrow. The field looks down
To an old quarry and road, and across
To a dark beach on the Atlantic.

Stone from the quarry built a small
Custom's House out on the Point.
Its old form is in ruin, now!   But bells are
Still heard out there just before dawn:
Their purpose must fade over the water . . .

The water knows the three formal elements
That should compose an ode: say it, *élan!*
There's turn and counter-turn . . .
And turn, again; not *stand!*
The epode has a talent for rattling a tambourine
Like pie-tins strung across a garden
To frighten, at night, the subtle, foraging deer.

The epode knows about fear; but, shaking
In its bones, I've said it has a talent for
Playing the tambourine by ear.
The raccoon struggling out of his tree
Doesn't care about
The eye, bait and teeth of a Windsor Trap;
The pie-tins, touched by a wind moving
Over the spears of corn, do not

Confuse him.
He wanders off into the orchard and down
Into a fast stream where suddenly
A grinning hound stops him—
The coon rears up on his haunches like a bear,
Spits and screams: his claws
At the weeping eyes of the big dog: turned twice,

The hound bites into fur, meat and *then*
Deep into the spilled milk of the spine. This is
When the stream seems empty, silent!
This is also where the story divides in my mind.
What can I tell you?
Only that in past centuries
There were fewer
Dimensions to any concept of time,
And there was a greater acceptance of mirrors, and rhyme.

Against the Wishbone

In March, hens roost in the throne room folded
In black and gold hampers. There are urns
Of water at both ends of the flowering troughs
Of window-boxes. The boughs of evergreen are
Like the large messed feathers of parrots, leaning

And diseased in their ivory cages. A servant
Opens the giant fire screen,
Its iron netting
With lavender and green dragons ascending
At its wings. This morning the King
Was suffering cramps, and as he sat

Before this stone hearth, a whole skeleton,
With a great weight of emeralds around its neck,
Dropped out of the chimney onto the flaming
Branches of apple, cedar and red hazel. *The King*

Had a very troubled day . . . I'm his troubled Queen!
At midnight there will be a banquet,
A juggler has raised along the wall a cloth backdrop
That is velvet with enameled planets, the moons
Are flecks of amber streaked with gold—
He'll juggle three burning clubs behind him, and

To the eye, they'll combine becoming one
Valiant circuiting sun! Another fat parrot drops

With a thud onto the straw and twine bottom
Of its cage. *Then there is silence again!*
In the tapestry above the table
A cobra climbs the air to show
How a feasting worm can turn on stairs
Of decaying vertebra:
A wild boar, its throat opened by dogs, is dead,
There, in the fabric, in the wet silvery woods . . .

The cottage in my dream of a cruel winter, at Blossom,
        details joy
And the crimson ink of berries like those red towers
Of coronation that begin a monk's otherwise serious
Squared lettering.
It seemed to me, after waking from the peasant's countryside

That the rebel angels are not waiting for the Spring:

I am still a child! My husband, the King,
Says that early April
Will lift the winter's quarantine . . . he and my mother
Are agreed that I must be his lover before the rains begin!
There's a black mole that's grown on my breast?
And I have dreamed of a terrible thing, a sea snail,
Large as a husband's fist, feeding in the cold
Atlantic shoals: its secret is that it submits,
It opens its one door, in intervals, to the full force
Of the ocean,
All the weight of the sea looping
Through a pink banked interior, the wonderful conjugal
Cup and spoon— the seawater turns
Like a peregrine in a strong reversal of wind, which lifts
        a cottage and walks it
Like an unwilling toad far into the virgin wilderness!

The Parallax Monograph
for Rodin

I dreamt, last night, of your stone cabinet, *Porte de l'Enfer*,
Everything was there, except it had turned into
The doors of an elevator in an old hotel of potted ferns. I'm certain
That outside the hotel there was a beach with, here and there, a colorful
But faded umbrella!   I said it wasn't changed, but that's not fair;
I hesitate to say this, but *the contemplative*, with his head
Resting on his fist, was replaced, in the dream, by a clock
That somehow told the time of day and the location of the elevator!
The face of all this work seemed unchanged, still a clamoring
Of naked men and women, not religious but ordered in their desperation.

My favorite figure remains: the woman on the far right just below
The strong backside of a man who's assisted in his climb: his left foot
Lifts from her extended left hand and arm—her hair cannot be
Described, omitted as if swept aside by a severe comb,
Her breast is young but not exactly firm.
I don't really know if she assists
The man above her or if this was just an opportunity he seized;
After all, his right foot rests on a head that has no body.
I sense their community as being *of oblivion*. Outside
This hotel elevator the unbaptized infants wait, unwashed and
Smoking green cigars, they are delayed, in limbo . . .

The dream has worked a parody of your dark, portal scene,
Deus ex machina, and your intense belief in a teeming life

That struggles for relief out of a slab of rock in which
You saw it all from the very beginning: helmets, wings, thighs,
Breasts, hands, ankles, mouths, and even the small cherub peeing
Into the cracked mirror. The mirror is the mouth of an obese banker
From Reims. Everything you made
Was placed in an enclosing but not final space. Only the most
Brilliant comedian possesses your gestures in their correct
Abstract mathematical sequence. I think by now

We must be alone!
My bored reader having just left us both for a fresh lettuce sandwich—
Sometimes abstraction suits me like throwing rocks
In a building with a simple clerestory of stained glass. *We should*
Discuss light. It has suggestive, serial properties like a girl's loud
Orgasm in a drifting rowboat over a peaceful river, at night.
Let's pretend the lovers in the rowboat have drifted for nearly
A kilometer, and now, at the moment that she announces
Her arrival at this thunder-struck height, her lover discovers
They have floated up to a dock filled with aristocrats
At a party with lap-dogs, wine and hanging lanterns . . .

The girl is sitting on the boy, the rowboat rocks gently.
The boy's nakedness is lost, made modest, by his partner's
Large thighs and buttocks, she
Is indifferent to the strangers on the dock; she goes on
Screaming the boy's name, and the rowboat drifts past the dock
Back into the shadows of the trees that contain the river.
Wonderful! The aristocrats are bent in stitches of laughter.

I was talking about your comical gestures, and an obscure thought
That discouraged my reader, who left for a sandwich. To punish
Him I have invented this charming vignette of pleasure which he's
        missed!
He thinks little of your materials: there's strings, wires, planes and
Cubes. The vertical sequences of nudes. You appraised a nude
Like a sturdy chair or stool.

The way you place Balzac's head in that massive unfinished neck,
His face is like a smashed gem in matrix.
The apprehension of chiaroscuro, as in the lines of a daffodil, is
Not your style. The princess, David, of Donatello is not your style!
Anything free-standing like a glutton in an English garden *is*
Your style.
The infants, unwashed, still smoking cigars, in front of your elevator,
Have begun a card game; they curse and spit but are not offensive.

Rodin, I've put off saying this, but your male secretary is sad
And disheartened . . .
He writes with power about the corpse on the kitchen table.
In triplicate, he's sent an application, listing grievances, to the stars!
He now operates your old elevator in that dream hotel.
He's left everyone in the lurch; ground level. What's he doing now
That instructs the summer guests to undress and climb the walls?
Tortured and naked, they seem to have little patience with him.
His name? The real key is silver on a chain streaming from his pocket.

Your secretary is on the roof of the hotel having a smoke
While looking out over the ocean.   He has been joined by two waiters.
They gaze out over the water, remembering the quiet
Days of the winter. You were smart
To have a poet as your servant in serious matters.
And what's more important than this closet on a string, the box that
Climbs vertically through the large, broken-down hotel, famous
For its spirits of bottled water!   One of the two
Waiters finishing his smoke becomes careless . . .
There are screams of *Fire, Fire!* My faithless reader
Done with his sandwich, and a lover of big fires, returns
And says: *What an inferno, they are all lost; poor souls!*
I have not guessed the secrets of your closet. But out on the Atlantic

A ship bobs up and down, a sailor
Looks over to land and sees the burning parallax beams of the hotel.

The sailor's brow is like marble . . . my reader in a trembling voice now
Speaks to the sailor, asking, "What's the matter, what's that
Fire on the shore?" The sailor answers,

"It's Hell, of course!"

The World Isn't a Wedding of the Artists of Yesterday

They were with me, and they were me . . .
As we all moved forward in a consonance
*   silent and moving,*
Seated and gazing,
Along the beautiful river forever.

—DELMORE SCHWARTZ

A stub of a red pencil in your hand.

A Georgia O'Keefe landscape rising beyond
The carcass of black larkspur,
Beyond the Milky Way where
The lights of galaxies are strung out over a dipper of gin
With a large sun and the rotund

Fuchsia moon. Her closet is empty, except for the manuscript
With your signature. She has left you!
Where was it in the field
That you threw the telephone:
After moving away
From the farmhouse, you found it again when
Returning for the lost cat—

As you walked through the low chinaberries calling
Her name you found the white horn
Of the telephone. You are alone calling to the frozen
Countryside of New Jersey.
She sleeps

In the yellow wicks of the meadow:
You are calling the mopsy cat back

From the ditch, but Dexedrine presses a pencil
Up against your eyebrow and temple. And
You've forgotten— *what was it?*

Out there in the field calling

Across the cold night air, drinking from the gold flask,
Again tucking that stub of a pencil
Back behind your ear. You read, this morning,
In the crisp pica lettering of the old Remington,
How boatmen navigated the winter shallows of the Seine
Guided by a lamp burning all night
In a narrow window in Flaubert's study;

And all of a sudden, under severe stars, beside water,
You remembered everyone who was a friend.

But why your hand is locked on a red pencil, again,
At the bottom of a wintry meadow, in New Jersey,

Is a mystery rising behind you on the wind . . .

The Land of Cockaigne: 1568

—homage to PIETER BRUEGEL, *the elder*

Below the hill, between a gorge and azure maritime horizon,
Is a trench of darkening cowslip, edelweiss
And burdock. Also, there's a village, north to south,
Amber like the light of the gospels: a fat goose
Is being shivered under the knife; children are playing
Knuckles in the square,
And there is the seal
Of a leper's annealed yellow mouth; two boys above him

Straddle a sooty stack of a chimney, they are
Topsy-turvy, winnowing feathers in a strong wind
That jumps the Protestant martyrs dangling
From gallows, the webs of cloudwheels, or
The rotten crossed-poles of a country crucifix. The Spanish

Inquisition stations horsemen in wine-red cloaks
Below these limestone sites of execution . . .
I have walked that stretch of the canal between the two
Green windmills. And, then, visited the tavern:

Christophe Plantin, friend to genius, and I
Are drinking through the night, his wife

Is unfaithful! I tell him that it is the times,
And to accept each betrayal as treaty: a gift

Of sitting under pines,
So sleepy that I might again
Be bleeding inside, below me on the sea
Ships are lighting fires in those big iron dishes
Made popular by the Greeks!
I leave Christophe for a pitcher of raw eggs in cream. The ulcer
Is otherwise treated with leeches!
The weddings of peasants become weird, golden

With an underpainting of desperation and taxes. Where are the magi?
Below the docked tree there are three men lounging—
A farmer, a scholar, and a knight. The collector, Niclaes Klaus,
Describes the three as inert petals, swollen with rain, but still
Sucking at the stalk—   that is not it!
They are just awkward skaters, in May,

Supported by a revolving
Vertical plane at the center of the painting.
They are foreshortened by the sensations of the morning, and
By Cockaigne.
To see their situation, you must first witness,
In grisaille, the burning of the diseased in the cities, or
The long massacre of children down a snowy lane, or even
The virgin in her quilted coat carrying in her pail
A landlord's gift, the surplus of fresh sudsy milk.
There will be a late Twelfth Night waffle
For each of her nine brothers and sisters . . .
King Philip's flesh-poles are made of silver poplars,
Felled, in October—   dragged like apostles
Through the slashing wheat fields of Flanders . . .

*

There are five vermillion figures on the pond. They glide
Across the ice toward the wooden chute of the Falls.

Snow lifts off the steeple, tumbling straight
Into the open mouths of children, who spin up
Against the masonry of the small chapel—
The funeral procession turns to the sea
Descending into the churchyard where an Elder

Stands with a blue candle that has melted
Entirely into its saucer, the flame blossoms,
Crosses the surface like a magpie pushed by a sudden breeze!
Christophe Plantin's

Suicide came on a dark, dark day. He had brewed
Henbane with the seeds of the Saint Ignatius bean.
His eyes were ribboned internally with bleeding . . .
I have never painted, I confess,

A female nude—   unless, you've inspected
My canvas of *Dulle Griet,* where just above
The black sickle moon, a nude couple, in summer,
Are sitting out on the water . . . they were the innocents.

Only two! Christophe must now be at liberty
To perch in snow on the hill
And peer down on us, on rooftops with their mud and stone

Pottles, in which the doves will roost.
I have gazed down the cows' path to the churchyard; there,
My friend lies in his lavender gravecloth . . .

Christophe,
Take with you the sweet scent of woodsmoke, burning
Bayberry and cedars, take the joyous light of December's noonday,

But, also,
Take with you, in your dark winnowing,
These red languishing silks of the joy of skating!

Empiricists of Crimson

*There seem to be only three alternatives to the
doctrine that perception is of the contemporary:
what we perceive (a) occurs only in our minds; (b)
is something projected by us on to an environing
void; or (c) is distant from us in space and time.*

—PAUL WEISS

We can distinguish through the mist a red parrot feather
On a conquistador's musket, the feather suggests
To him the direction and force of the equatorial winds;
His broad cape flutters and then lifts into the orange sunset, a single
Ball smashes through two pears in a twisted tree. Below him
Is the jungle gorge with its waterfall and dark lake—
The expedition like a ribbon of smoke climbed all day
Up the slippery green wall of this abyss, the youngest
Of the infected officers fell backwards, growing smaller
And smaller, his brains like rope following him into the water.
His scream was lost to the deafening waterfall.   His fellow soldiers
Are lost to their progress up through fog.
A panther watched the Spaniard tumble down the rocks to his death,
It drank
Again from the muddy lake. A priest, high up in the nimbus,
Wrote in his diary that the black cat then raised his lustrous head
To sniff the air for blood as if there had been
No loss, just its consequence—

                              as if red meat had been dropped
Down to him by a superfluous god
Way above him on the rock and moss steps that climb
Into the clouds . . .

In the middle of the night the priest, himself delirious with fever,
Made a last entry in his diary: *my companion, Carlos, and I*
Did as you wished, Mother; we are in the New World and
The shape of a pear is something that does not perish
For it suggests the space that
The pear occupies; suggests its flavor, there in the mind, but
Without any regard to time—back in Madrid, in my father's house,
The Queen's mummers are blowing their trumpets, announcing Easter.
Shade is the sanctuary of pears! The mummer's wear conical hats, and
                              turn as
My mind turns in fever; if you are handed this diary by my Captain,
You'll understand. My best contemporary and I are slain. The shape of
A pear is an adventure of space which neglects in the mind
All murmurs and mimes, all red lines of conquest. And

                              in a niche of time, our young friend, Carlos,
Was devoured, Mother, by a big cat the exact color of your eyes . . .

There Is a Dream Dreaming Us

For THOMAS JAMES

We are seven virgins.   Seven lamps.
Each with a different animal skin on our shoulders.
We had crowns made of black mulberry with the pyracantha,
Its white flowers in corymbs spotted with yellow fruit.
On my forehead, in charcoal, is the striking digit
Of an asp, and with all of this we were nearly nude.

The procession to the pyramid began at the pavilion
At the very edge of the thirteen acres that were sacred.
We walked ahead of everyone with our priest,
But we are the last to leave this world for the portico
And the first gallery which is dark and cold.

We stood on the terraced face of the pyramid witnessing
The long entrance of the king's family.
The queen carried a lamb made of papyrus: its eyes
Were rubies. The Queen's brother was dressed

In little rattles made of clay.
Even the King's nursery followed him with two slaves
To the chamber where we would all stay.
The sun no longer touched us on the plateau. It was lost

Making the sand dunes beyond the cataract rise and fall
Like water rushing toward us.
The glass doll was smashed above the portico,
And the doors began to close! We were inside the galleries
Of sun and flour and our seven lamps guided us
To the underground chamber. We could no longer hear
The drums leaving the inner acre.
I am the initial lamp and so I broke the last bottle

And from the bottle sand poured:
This last gate had two flanking chambers full with sand
And on it was the weight of marble columns,
Columns that joined the limestone slab that was
The last seal lowering now as the sand spills
Into two fern boxes on the floor.

The children had all been smothered and washed in oils,
All of the family is poisoned.
They sprawl around the sarcophagus which is open.
The priest has stabbed my six companions—it is
A noise like a farmer testing river soil.
I'm to drain the cup of wine that the King's mother
Handed me before dying. I was the *first lamp,* but
This is my story. I spilled the wine down my leg
And pretended to faint away. The priest thinking everyone
Had crossed from his world stopped his prayer. He walked
To the girl with the third lamp.
He kissed my dead sister on the lips. He ripped the silk
From her breasts. And then he fell on her.
Her arms were limp, I imagine even as they would be
If she were alive doing this with him.

The heat must have been leaving her body. He, finishing,
Turned to me: what I saw was the longest
Of the three members of an ankh, all red, and from it
Came a kind of clotted stream.

But his strength was leaving him visibly; he put his
Dagger in his neck and bled down his sleeve.
I don't understand. But now

I am alone as I had planned.
I'm a girl who was favored in the market by the King.
I've eaten the grapes that the slaves carried in for him:
If someone breaks into this tomb in a future time how
Will they explain the dead having spit grape seeds
Onto a carpet that was scented with jasmine?
The arrogance of the living never had a better monument
Than in me. I am going to sleep
In a bed that was hammered out of gold for a boy
Who was Pharaoh and King of Egypt. My father died free.
My mother died a slave, here, at this site after being
Whipped twice in a morning. In the name of Abraham

I have displaced a King. I picked him up
And put him in the corner, facing in and kneeling.
He would seem to be a punished child.
What he did? I will tell you; you will be told many times again:

He killed four thousand of my people
While they suffered the mystery of this mountain appearing
Where there was nothing but moving sands and wind!

The Scrivener's Roses

For MARVIN FISHER

The gulls fly in close formation becoming a patch of sail . . .
They divide revealing a blue patch of sky. They dive
At a gun-carriage on which the dead cot-boy writhed
Much of last night. It is a flight of seagulls
Above the drying cannon-brooms that makes the bay
Seem at all alive. It is over the dead water that the surgeons
Come:

over the bay American ships of war give up
Their cutters, the handsome surgeons climbing
Into rowboats and transported to the flag-ship where
The Surgeon of the Fleet chews patiently on beefsteak within this dark, dry
Man-of-War. They will gather for an amputation:
On dressers an orderly arranges saws and knives, sponges
And tincture of iodine, the hooked darning-needles are beside
The yellow bee's-wax and thread. One boy is dead, another
Is barely alive. The oldest surgeon's face
Is white with scarlet brands like the ash-hole in sickbay
With its few *live* red coals in a deep pan. The sawing on
The mahogany femur of the thigh is trying for the aging physician.
The leg will be hidden from sight behind a wood pile.
Across the bay on the beach a dark flamingo, in ridicule, stands
On just one leg. And a bugle signals
The return of the cutters to their separate ships.

The two dead boys are from New England. What had they endured?
They often said that an April snow was a poor man's manure.
Their sisters work in Carson's Old Paper Mill. The youngest girl
Worked a Tymer-press, an iron machine that drops a weighted, sunken
Impression of roses onto a soft, scented stationery.
Two of the sisters have died in the mill, mauled by machinery!
The sleighs that are usually loaded with paper carried their bodies to
The cemetery on the hill.

Their distant cousin, Herman Melville, attended both burials.
He said to their mother, "Ruth, you still have a husband, two boys
At sea, and Elizabeth who'll soon marry. That Baker's-stove
The girls gave to me flared up last week, scorching my study window.
The window now is like a Claude-glass; it frames the river and snowy
    fields
While giving them the golden lights of the Claude Lorrain landscape. I'll
Remember the girls each time I stare through the panes
Of that almost amber window!"

Leaving his cousins, Melville on a train studies a passing meadow:
He has never before seen Jacks-in-the-pulpit flowering
In snow, standing in a late Spring snow! He felt that the meadow
Was a white necropolis with toppled towers like halves of eggshells
After the weasel has raided the hen-house.
He wondered if black ants were dead inside the walls
Of this wide, tufted city? He longed for the hearth.
For cider bottles popping in the cellar. For muffins with honey!

He will visit a small branch of The Dead Letter Office in Washington:
A large house with bare rooms, five rooms in the round, and
Each has a fireplace leading to a common, federal chimney. Five clerks
Wrapped in scarves stand before their assigned fire. They open
The letters spilling coins and rings into a steamer trunk. There are
The thin silver rings for children; rings of engagement for fingers
    already

Tattered to the bone like masts of a ghost ship under an opaque moon.
      These letters
Spoke of affection, luck fishing for trout, of drought, of the deaths
Of this and that rich uncle. Five clerks at each fire, five fires!
      The black
Smoke rises from the single great stack, and a shopgirl across
The street in her attic room writes a letter describing the smoke as
      it drifts
Out over Washington to the bay and woods. She writes on scented sheets

To her brother who is at sea. He died in February. She is run over
That evening by a wagon loaded with raw cotton. Herman Melville stood
Over her in the street.

                              Just above her blue stocking, above
      the blue garter
Is a wound in her thigh and a spurting artery, horse manure
And young active flies . . .

Walking back to the hotel he decides to return to his home by Friday,
He'll sit on the North porch and write and heal, the North porch
Like a sleety deck of a ship where the Captain is lashed to the wheel . . .

That Appius Claudius failed to drain the Pontine marshes is similar,
He believes, to this government's failure to burn all the dead letters
Of just a single week! He feels they could simply be scattered like gulls
                from the crow's-nests of ships out
                    on the open sea!

                   *

The convent is in ruin. The churchyard is a basin filled with graves and
It extends into the adjacent park where farmers are chopping down trees
So as to be able to dig more graves late that evening. Sherman's
      artillery
Has destroyed the joists and center beam of
The convent, killing fifty-three nuns and an old priest. The farmers cut

Down trees and the birds and red squirrels are fleeing to the stream that
Is beside the old Saw Mill and its livery . . .
The next afternoon the Union soldiers enter the town, they lose the light

Of day while looting and drinking. At dusk, searching for women, they
Arrive at the churchyard—with bayonets they open the fresh mounds
Where the sisters were hurriedly buried. Lanterns are strung up
In the few standing trees, the cook plays his red accordion, and
The men in their blue caps and jackets are dancing clumsily with
The dead women who have been stripped to the waist; their white bibs
And black birdcloth veils littering the green bowl of the dim churchyard:
Out of the mouths of the jostled corpses falls grave soil and
Ivory crowns from teeth. The dancing soldiers are laughing

With their rigid partners in moonlight, you can hear dry bones
Breaking! Some of the women are shaven, one has long red hair.
Their white breasts bouncing in the chill night air. Behind the hedge
Of the churchyard three black children hide while sobbing.
They understand these free men grinning through beards,
Drinking whiskey; one falling back into an empty grave.
Two sergeants, who are yet boys, are undressing the gray-haired
Mother Superior . . .

In this judgment the dead climb out of their shallow places
And waltz—all but three are now completely naked!
There are haloes of cigar smoke over the struggling couples.
The nun with red hair is young and freckled with a bloodless bayonet
Wound in her neck. One of her eyes is bruised shut; the other is
Open, ice-green and resigned. A bonfire is started.

You can hear hammers striking rail down by the depot.

The severe ebony and pearl garments of the sisters are thrown
On the fire. And what we know

Is that in the morning these soldiers, in a line three deep,
Moved on through Georgia for the sea . . .

*

The Chinese creeper climbing over lilac beside the piazza
Is infested with worms. The swing
On the piazza is nudged by wind, and Melville
Empties his pipe against the stone drain.
On the porch, at sunset, he trembles a little
Both in act and shadow,

Memento mori . . . the Antigone of paper, who dropped her sweet, iron
Roses onto thin polished sheets, is dead; but her sister, Elizabeth,
Is alive and has
Written from Washington to their brothers, the sailors;

They have been buried in a tropical cemetery for paupers and pilgrims.
Elizabeth has accidentally rented a room across
From the house to which her letter will be delivered.
She has told her brothers there will not be civil war.
She enclosed a watercolor miniature that depicts nuns bent in labor
In a sunny cotton field in Georgia.
And up the federal chimney goes this gesture of an ordinary, occult
Shopgirl. The genius of her vigil mixes ashes with ashes,
Tears with tears, and ink with the long white fabric of paper . . .

A fisherman
Out at sea held a packet of seeds and wished he'd hear
The madness of roosters as he neared the land and long beaches.
The winter beaches with their snowy dunes, white on white, or

Memento mori . . . the crisp depression of a clear rose
On its clear stem. This perfumed impression in the corner of a
        crême paper
Is our lesson in understanding him: Melville dreamed he was

At sea in a state-cabin which was sealed and calked for an eternal
Crossing of the Atlantic. There are mice
In the desk drawers. Dust everywhere. And large linens
Draped over the furniture and mirrors.
It was like the mystery of an ancient scroll.
It was losing your soul down the awful mouth of a newborn, the perfect
Mouth spitting breast milk, while the infant in coarse swaddling
        is bricked-up

                                    inside the monastery's south garden wall.

TWO

Well—I made you take time to look at what I saw and when you took time to really notice my flower you hung all your own associations with flowers on my flower and you write about my flower as I think and see what you think and see of the flower—but I don't . . . so you want me always to paint flowers.

—GEORGIA O'KEEFE

The Everlastings

In the village it must be a clear night with the light of a red
Star twisting down the water
Filling the distant mouth of our narrow fjord . . .

Snow blankets the sleeping mustard, thistle and gorse!

Two longships have been brought up on forms:
Their bellies are checkered with tar and goatskins.
The wind is up in the bones.   The dogs
Are peaceful.   I have died
On a beach in France.   A monk
And I did battle.   I wish I could burn the little icon
Of the nut-fairy; its red berries in the triangular seed-box
And the roof of furze and maple.   It was a gift
From the King, my father.   Tonight, here in the water I feel
Closer to my mother . . .

    In the frescoes
    Of the lives of the saints, there's hibiscus, rhubarb
    And roses sketched on wet plaster, each flower
    Outlined by a fine bone pencil, and when the lime

    Touches the air the watercolors
    Become thin, speckled—

A daubing of light
In the cobwebs suspended between a stag's antlers.
Saint Odoacer, our fourth pope, brought to the lepers
The fanaticism of the rose
With its old, unfolding characteristics of fire.

He embalmed the Viking's daughter,
Scooping out her breads and heart: in their place
He laid sticks of balsam with salt.
He put spices inside her skull.
He sat her in a jar with the knees snapped, brought back
Under her jaws.

The jar filled with wild, languorous honey!

My stomach is opened. My sword fell at the Viking's collar,
Leaving the body above the silver braided waist—
Arm and shoulder dropping into the surf.

The moon sits on my shield, lighting the circle
Of oxskulls
Which the goldsmith staggered, every third one, with
Delicately hammered suns . . .

My daughter's womb was put in an ark of osier and sedge;
Taken out over the waters in a votive ship . . .
On my shield, at the center of the oxskulls, there is
A silver wreath, all of this worked into its carapace
That is the brine-soaked shell of a sea-tortoise. I cracked the Pope's
Skull with it. I have scattered his monks!
I no longer dream of long oars breaking up
In the drifting lakes of kelp. The loadstone,
In its sock of pig intestine, spins to the south? Not Odin
Calling? The fingers of the fog are white like every ninth wave
Across our bow.

My daughter was born in a pine forest in mid-summer.

To die at dawn is to wash down with hot ale the raw red livers
Of sea-turtles. *Is to smile at my father!* What I feel
Is not fear, it's more the sudden circumspection
Of deer just before they follow the white roebuck who leaps
Over horizons.

      HAIL NORTHMAN! HOW IS IT? No, he'll think that
      I'm taunting him. He could be free in the tides? There was blood
      All over him and sea foam like the saliva of wild dogs.
      His beard stood in the sun like laden papers
      Of honeycomb. In the lives of the saints there are red stars,
      And one is painted over another, crossing out the eyes
      Of the unicorn and lion. The Norsemen thought the frescoes
      Were secret maps to the Underworld, and they'll voyage anywhere:

      They have pulled oars while caught in maelstroms. They filled
      Sails while being dragged down into the blood-sworls
      Of their thumbs. I love their pandemonium. Listen—

It is the thunder at dawn!

The Sketchbook Ashes
of Jehoshaphat

—ROBERT LOWELL, 1917–1977.

A painter, thin with auburn hair, works before an easel
While looking coldly into a meadow, her free hand
Raises the red gauze of her dress to scratch a pink
Spider bite that isn't there, up where the leg emerges
From the soft shadow of draping buttock muscles—

She'll do the meadow over tomorrow
With even more ghostly silica orbs of dandelions, adding the red
        spouting
Indian-pipe and tacit buttercups;
Water wells up in the painter's mouth and she swallows it . . .

Earlier in the morning, with a similar unconscious gesture,
You skimmed cream off a saucer of bread in milk, the cream
Was like petals of a buttercup
Caught in a wooden spoon, these mustard-colored flowers are shyly

Acquired by the canvas, and with that exact, same gesture
Of skimming milk . . .

The painter's black dog jumped up out of the meadow,
His jaws snapping at the air-borne fleets of the wandering dandelion—

Each seed is a fading cipher
Like the invincible, numinous finger of a Balinese dancer . . .

The day of your death, a limousine will enter the cemetery
Beyond the river; there are rolling lawns landscaped with pine
And willow.

And the dead are like the nude with small breasts who poses
For students! She has knowledge of the difficult, imperceptible
Rehearsals of weight that make you steady as statuary; adjustments
Of weight, the penciled-in lines of your legs, in relationship
To your hips, which the students will justify by inches—
                             using the very last crumbs of their erasers . . .

And the large flapping sheets of paper are pinned by their elbows, as
One sketch after another is wasted, torn away and tossed up into the air
Of this cold room with its big sweeping mirrors, the nude with auburn hair
Has a white vaccination on her thigh beside a fresh spider bite,
        the instructor
Touches a clear cube of ice to the bite while he stutters, apologizing:
                             she steps back into her black robe, looks
Above herself to the silk hammocks of speckled brown spiders; what she
        observes
Is the first principle of weight in suspension
                             which separates the heavy cream while lifting
It to the surface, then skimming
The meadow like a breeze that carries you and the dandelion seeds into
The oblivion of the next season, *where limp*

Long greens of dandelion boil through a steamy, summer evening . . .

Telemachos Who Believes
Ulysses Is the Night

It is like bathwater in which a prince has been slain, the sunrise

Weights everything as if each ray of light
Had draped on it
The drying skins of lizards. The pink light is intensified, bent
In the tips of waves. I have a piece of charcoal for a plaything.
A gull drops balancing a lump of gold on each wing! It is Athena
Come to visit me. She understands voyage is a pastime . . .
By now the women of Ithaca are out working in the quarries. Helios will

Bless them. Beware of smoke rising above a coppice of bushes and trees.
A sanctuary of pigs and deer. He sat in Circe's tub to drain a boil
Which appeared on his sunken abdomen after a meal of foul mussels.
I fear that she spits silk out over the grasses at evening! Our ship

Rolls to the north as it crests the wave, and the lamp
Strikes the pomanders, spraying cloves
All over the heated stones I had just placed
On wet reeds. I try to ease my breathing with steam. I wanted to describe
A sunrise, at sea.
It's like bleeding from the eyebrow!
It is the water-clock from Rhodes that belonged to my mother:

The water, tinted lavender, is made to flow in tears
From the eyes of automata—a floating figure, who falls through

The shadows of twilight, who points to the passing hour
With its pink symbol painted on the twisting glass tower of this
Clepsydra, louvered by my father for my mother. Now, though,
It's the middle of the night; I can hear the raked sails
Of the *Dreadnought* straighten, again
Like oarsmen, who in one motion fly forward
With their oars, as if to destroy the accomplishment
Of rowing—to which the moment

Of flying forward is engaged
As night is to a desire for the silk transparency of day!

The Circus Ringmaster's
Apology to God

It is what we both knew in the sunlight of a restaurant's garden
As we drank too much and touched
While waiting for the lemon wedges and rainbow trout.
If it's about that door? I'm not sorry.
You smiled through tears. The night clerk said that I was
Crazy like a bear. Laughing, you spilled your beer.

Over the hedge a farmer paints a horse's cankers
With a heavy tincture of violet . . .

Later, in a dark room, both of us speckled, middle-aged and soft,
I dragged my mouth like a snail's foot up your leg and body
To your mouth. We both shivered.
You ran naked before a window. Shyness increases your importance!

I don't know what you think when we are no one for a moment:
Hay-ropes, hands at ankles, gone beyond
Even the dripping faucet and its sink spilling onto the floor . . .

There's no strongbox hidden in the closet.

It's often like laughter, "You go pee for me and I'll boil the water."
Sipping hot coffee, you told me a story about the old ringmaster
On the Baltic shore:

he's inside his little house on wheels, and
The goldfinch jumps from its silver platform to the cage's floor that's
Littered with straw and shredded handbills. The ringmaster daydreams
About ponies circling in a white path of ashes . . .
On the table before him there's an ounce of tobacco
And in his plate: blue and gray parsnips, beef and the opened letter

That he knows better than the loose floorboard! The two of us
Enjoy our solitude:
                                    folded over chairs are the clothes
We never wore. If you die first, I'll sway in the hallway like a bear.
            I'll whisper, "I'm sorry". And you'll
Not unlock the door.
I'll break through with my hip and shoulder . . .
Remember? You were glad that I did it once before!

Comes Winter, The Sea Hunting

For HANNAH

This was your very first wall, your crib against
The wall that was papered in a soft
Fawn-color, the powdered wings of a moth
Slowing in the cobwebs of the window—

The moth, poor like us, died
In her paper dress on stilts. The spider
Is a monarch, fat in
Winter chambers, the articles of her
Wealth are also
The articles of the kill: a little narcotic with silk!

We had two rooms in a blue, collapsing roadhouse
At the very lip of a valley
With a deep river and woods. The house
Had been settling for a century.
Those dizzying, tin
Trapezoid rooms . . .
A house built on rock, a rock built on sand,

And while I slept, your mother, who was
Big with you, hammered from silver—

A knife! A spoon! You,
On a crescent of bone, sleep
A sleep of plums: moisture on the plum forms a window

And inside everything reclines tasting meat and wine
From mid-day
Until evening. *That winter came in terms of you* . . .

The wet pods on sticks, mimes playing
Dice in a blizzard! Out of fields of rice come women
From the North, dark pajamas full of explosives . . .
Your mother now is
Naked and dreaming in the corner,
Is the Elder Bruegel's inverted, golden doe
On a green pole, being
Shouldered back to the winter village.

Inside a box by the stairs there's an egg
Halved by a hair,
A box filled with sleep, and even the retired ferryman,
George Sharon, leaving
Us two bottles of milk in the morning,
Would not look into it!
The cedar balcony in the back took on its weight

In ice. First, just three large icicles, then five,
And finally a webbing in between of thin ice.
The balcony was sealed
In a wall of crystals. With your new spoon
I carved into this blue-green wall

Durer's *Sky-map*
Of the Northern Hemisphere: the silver, ancestral
Figures of crab, spectacle bear,
And *Boötes* with his long pink muscles and spear:

On clear nights the opaque stars above Montpelier
Appeared through this Sky-chart.

Up in the corner, where
'the fish with spilled pitcher' should be,
There was instead
A bat, snow had
Brought the roof in on him and he was
Caught in ice, hanging by a claw in the eaves.

I called him
Pipistrelle, old and dead flittermouse, he was
A reach of bone and a square of fur like a squirrel
Nailed out on a red barn in October. Pipistrelle,
At the corners of his wings, had blackened stars. Valiant

Durer's Sky-map
Was now different with these triangular ears—
The dead pipistrelle carries a sound-picture
That is like our memory of the dark trees, or the spaces
Between the old ferryman's teeth.
The bat would use its wings
Like oars; rowing in the blackish cataracts
Of a winter porch: star-room! Lamp-room . . .

The winter comes,

A sea hunting, and your father after sleeping
Put his fist into the star-wall, making a hole;
The wind entered

Moving at the height of the unborn,
This wind erased the lights of hemispheres!
That night, a breaking of ice, and the next morning
The bag-of-waters begins seeping as your
Mother tries a flight of stairs—

An old woman puts a horn to her stomach, and
Listens for you,

You have formed from seawater:
A deep luminous eye, digits, a bridge for a nose—
Abstract, monstrous— you have two oars!
You can only hear the ferryman in the cove,
Walking with his ladder, he somehow hangs his lamp
On the tall pole.

In an earlier season,

You were conceived, touched by *two* sounds of water
In a gulf; you formed your pulse, little patch over nothing,

Drawn in and drawn out— this is the meaning as,
Sadly and much later, a feather
Or candle is put to our mouths!

There were
Agates on the windowsill and a vase of dry pussywillows;

The out-larged map-maker's instruments boiling
Before labor, the towels and basins:
A hatching
In the ruby rhomboidal rooms where

A spider on her lucent thread
Swings into sunlight, then leaves us, climbing up
A silken helix to eaves and

Pigeon gloom. But

You have washed up in the surf, and look out over
A new light like water showing,
Another mother,

A first attempt for someone loved, as
Out of her dress dropped in a circle—   this nude,
The steady spectre at your birth,
Steps near to kiss you, circle of goldsmith's blue;
The pipistrelles fan the air . . .
This world would deceive us

So live in it as two! This was the very first wall
                        that you had to have passed through . . .

Coleridge Crossing
the Plain of Jars: 1833

For SHEROD SANTOS

The gypsies carry sacks of walnuts out of the groves.
A dog
Whimpers below the cemetery, near to the peat field.

With regard to color primarily, but also
Scent and form,
The browsing deer under the sycamores
Have the very properties of a peach
Spoiled on the branch by a blanketing frost . . .

The deer, in Asia,
Rise out of fog as though it were a pond.

I walk. And over the wind, I hear the crushing
Of talc for the shaping of a death mask. Why is it?

Young Keats is lost!

Joseph Severn's hurried sketch of the rouged corpse
Was like that deep violet thumbprint, this morning,
In the soft breast of the goose
Hung in a draughty printshop of my publishers!

Sarah watched from her window above the philodendron
While I crossed against the West Wind
Through the drifting snow. She lost sight of me
For a moment. She guessed I was again wrestling
The angel.
I did die there, briefly, in the blizzard
As I had once with my mother as a boy—
The first of April, nude except for our canvas shoes,
We stepped
Under the bitter waterfall fed with a run-off of snow.

My brain empties

As it will when I've stood under the compass
Of a great low chandelier, weighted
In the purity
Of vertical tiers of burning citron candles.

The gypsies' bonfire climbs the stone face
Of the nunnery . . .
A Christmas pie, already sampled by the children,

Sits on the cleared table.
I stepped into the parlor, and Sarah said, "I thought
The elements had swallowed you
Just as you passed the last sycamore?"

She smiled in her chair, from half-dark,
And sewed—
I knew the chipped fire of pond ice
Was in her eyes like a widow's soul.

Principia Mathematica:
Einstein's Exile in
an Old Dutch Winter

My theory withstood the light of the Hyades

While it passed our darkened sun. The eclipse
Was captured in Brazil and West Africa.
Here, at night, over the fields
The straight edge and compass become the severe poplar
And snowy tar-tipped spruce of Holland.
At this hour, I miss Berlin!
Descartes, too, once sat here washing oysters in milk,
The oysters of Leyden,
Laying them out over a bowl of snow,
Sprinkling pepper
Into the milk in its deep saucer,

A young mathematician
At the interior
Of a silver and gold mirror filled
With a watercolorist's impression
Of smokefall in winter.

There exists an imaginary plane, made
Increasingly solid with distance,
Like the weathered mechanical wings

Of a windmill, four pine blades
Becoming eight, becoming a bald porcelain face
In the amethyst shade
Of a cloudbank passing between sun
And the broken reeds of the lake.

Outside Leyden,
The wind is the lamp of projection!

Descartes, wintering with the armies
Of the Duke of Savoy, sat in his large furs
On the blazing bank of the Danube
Lecturing young bowmen, crying
That all of the pleasure of mathematics
Was in the one smooth pebble of *the calculus*.

There exists a flower, in Holland,
Which is not a member
Of the tremendous family of roses—
A flower which *is*, regardless,
The rose of all roses . . .

When the arrow passed through the fist
Of Cardinal Richelieu, he was dressed
In the red glove of his office; we would have said
His wound was discrete
And continuous
Like the brown burn of a canker on a rosebud.
My son has suffered a nervous breakdown!

He and I watched, in Venice, beside the old *Coq d'Or*—
In the vast relief of an exotic poverty, a barge's
Cargo of poppies was sucked down
Making sentient a geometry of water. I dreamt
Later of this vortex, in Pasadena,
In a closing circle which grew smaller,

More concentrated, until all the flowers
Fell through the bottom of their concentration
Opening into a siamese twin: two cones, black
Shifted to red, of infinite dimension—

If I enter myself with all the dignity
Of nature I will never come out again.

Descartes, in the windmill, grabbed linen
And a tarnished mothy spoon,
Sipped his peppered milk, studying himself
In the deep running mirror . . .

First light will enter his room like the powder-blue
Lepidoptera of Spring, come
To visit the mathematician
Who'll, now, sleep until evening dreaming
The triadic stream where
The opened breastbone of a swan
With its pier-and-lintel bones is like the window
Which contains the wintry reflection
Of the setting sun:

A waking Descartes, his red beard and smock,
Gazes out of the inferno of his window—
He is thinking of the transformative nature
Of light and symbol, he proposes

That the wasp nest up in the eaves on the windmill
Resembles the dead blossom on the lilac hedge.
Descartes is waking, he remembers the woes,
And the downcast eyes
Of his dear friend, the exiled Princess Elizabeth—
Again, in flight from emotion, he proposes . . .

The rose of all roses!

Lord Myth

A shadow through the room, a rising
Fan of violets, phenomenon
With scent, weighted with one Victorian

Iris: her long finger passes
Through the velvet drawer
Where the children's salt crystals
Are seeding along soft black threads.

In moving candlelight, still solemn,
She turns to him
And with the effort of a faint pilgrim,

At twilight, opening great barn doors
He opens her robe. She turns, he moans. There's

A rill of breast milk, a sudden sequence
Magically appearing in the deep specimen drawer.

The raven above her, on top of the oak breakfront,
Flies across the room, dragging its long tether
To the arm of the sofa. She is silent.
He whimpers.

The marble andirons cool and snap—
A pulse in the fat red crest between them.
The sun
Has set between the cliffs: inland,
And hounds are chasing something
Big across a wet sloping lawn . . .

The raven's descent to the sofa
Snuffed the storm-candle, carbon
Spackling the high ceiling above her—

A black feather plunges through the spiraling smoke.

After Spring Snow,
What They Saw

There are thirty-six folds to nothing—
Picture a holy man being eaten by two tigers.
The lovers are one white candle of procession
Descending the terraces of the winter garden.
She opens her mouth to the snowfall.
His knee
Is blue against her shadowed breast.
She arches her back
Grasping the pillow
And in the continuous light
Deer clatter past her, swerve
Up the rocks to the gorge . . .

His mouth, also, is open to darkness
While the large star-polyhedra
Of a cold interior
Float down over the two lovers
Like individual snowflakes into black water.
A rabbit scurries
And snow drops from the bough, a snare
Of juniper berries startling the cows,
The naked young couple
Are watched by an owl in a yew tree.
The man is weighted

Across the axis of the bed, one candle
Of procession brushing him
Under the spidery, marble pendentives . . .
Red maple leaves
Rush from a tree like blood .
Leaving the charred muscle that stops
First in her, first in him!

Rats circle over the translucent panels
Of the ceiling . . .
An archer in a big hood stands
With his back to falling water, the rail
Of his crossbow
Slamming back against his chest,
Which shallows, releasing its held breath:
The arrow recedes
Past its vanishing point in the icy falls.

There are large mirrors, half-buried
In the snow: in summer, they collect dew.
The mirrors are concave sheets of pink mica,
Burnished glass or jagged silver meteorites
Gathered over the generations.
This is the night of the great snail
Who has buried itself under decayed leaves
And black soil; painfully, months ago,
It dragged in its toe and heavy lime capstone.

The dead in their mud houses below the gorge
Sleep in the cinnabar stream
Of a winding sheet. They know
Her warm tears flow over his mouth, flowing
Into the hollows of her shoulders
And down over the frozen stepped stones

Of the enchanted garden where the russet hood
Of the poacher

Is visible, then, is not.
The owl thought
The young couple from above
Were like the poacher's dozen caged doves—
Wild inscribable wings attempting flight
Or, like the couple, love . . .

Not the Cuckold's Dream

For SAM PEREIRA

He lifts the white skiff up onto the beach. It is Easter.
He hears the tin bells of the peninsula. A storm coming?
Two torches smudge, then,
In the blue night, burn cleanly again . . .
The pearl slapdash of the moon

Is on the water. He lifts a flying fish
By its pink underwing, hurriedly snipping
With his teeth the last bloodblisters
Like a string of peppers ripe across his fingers.

At the ropeladder, he pauses and sits on the cold sand
To rub life into his feet.
He rinses his infected hands in the fire of bound cat-tails;

The fisherman touches the ladder of maguey flesh, and
Pulls up!
Swaying, he is like a gull's shadow
Climbing on thermals before the white cliff. The tide

Will follow behind him, rising in storm
It shatters the long skiff against the red adobe henhouse.

His strong, dark wife, a giantess, thought it was personal.
She comes out waving, in hysteria, a handkerchief.
She loses her laughter to a stitch. The wind taken from her:

She is knocked back and then down
By the falling water. The heavy pleated dress

Washes over her ashen face. She wishes
He had learned to swim.
There is a feeling of needles in her legs. He told

Her about the sea. *The sea is always feeding.*
The blood of his blistered hands is in his hair.
The fisherman raises dry bread to his mouth.

If I do not drown, *he thought of the father,*
I will marry, *he thought of the fish. . . .*

A Note on the Author

Norman Dubie was born in Barre, Vermont, in April 1945. His poems
have appeared in many magazines including *The Paris Review*, *The New
Yorker*, *The American Poetry Review*, *Antaeus*, *The Missouri Review*, and
Poetry. For his work, he has won the Bess Hokin Award of *Poetry* and a
fellowship from the John Simon Guggenheim Memorial Foundation. *The
Everlastings* is his eleventh collection of poetry. He lives in Tempe,
Arizona, with his daughter, Hannah. Mr. Dubie is a member of the
English Department at Arizona State University.